Edinburgh Clarendon Historical Society

The Clarendon Historical Society's Reprints.

Series III - 1866-88

Edinburgh Clarendon Historical Society

The Clarendon Historical Society's Reprints.
Series III - 1866-88

ISBN/EAN: 9783337252762

Printed in Europe, USA, Canada, Australia, Japan

Cover: Foto ©ninafisch / pixelio.de

More available books at **www.hansebooks.com**

"INTER FOLIA FRUCTUS."

THE
CLARENDON
HISTORICAL SOCIETY'S
REPRINTS.

SERIES III. 1886—88.

"History is but the unrolled Scroll of Prophecy."
—James A. Garfield.

EDINBURGH:
PRIVATELY PRINTED FOR THE SOCIETY.

This Edition is limited to 120 *large paper, and* 400 *small paper copies, for Subscribers only.*

INDEX.

	Page
I. Seditious Preachers, Ungodly Teachers.	1
II. The Massacres of Saint Bartholomew.	49
III. An Ordinance appointing Commissioners for approbation of Publique Preachers.	65

"Inter Folia Fructus."

SEDITIOUS

𝔓reachers,

UNGODLY

TEACHERS.

"History is but the Unrolled Scroll of Prophecy."
—James A. Garfield.

PRIVATELY PRINTED
FOR THE CLARENDON HISTORICAL SOCIETY.

1887.

This edition is limited to 120 large paper, and 400 small paper copies, for Subscribers only.

SEDITIOUS PREACHERS, UNGODLY TEACHERS.

EXEMPLIFIED,

In the Cafe of the Minifters, Ejected by the Act of Uniformity 1662, who appear to have been the only 𝕿𝖗𝖚𝖒𝖕𝖊𝖙𝖘 to 𝖂𝖆𝖗, and 𝕴𝖓𝖈𝖊𝖓𝖉𝖎𝖆𝖗𝖎𝖊𝖘 towards 𝕽𝖊𝖇𝖊𝖑𝖑𝖎𝖔𝖓, from their own Printed Sermons, and My Lord *Clarendon*'s Hiftory.

Oppofed chiefly to Mr. *Callamy's Abridgment*, where he has Canonized them for fo many *Saints* and *Confeffors*, to the great Encouragement of all Thofe, who fhall ever after Act by, and Avow the like Rebellious Principles and Practices.

Ex Ore tuo.

If the Perfon, and the Place, can improve and aggravate the Offence (as without doubt it doth, both before God and Man) methinks the Preaching Treafon and Rebellion out of the Pulpits, fhould be worfe than the advancing it in the Market, as much as poyfoning a Man at the Communion would be worfe than Murthering him at a Tavern. *Clarendon*'s Hift. of Rebell. Vol. 2. p. 19.

The *Independents* and *Prefbyterians* were equally Mafters of Diffimulation, and had equally Malice and Wickednefs in their Intentions, tho' not of the fame kind, and were equally unreftrained by any Scruples, or Motions, of Confcience. *Ibid.* Vol. 3. p. 82.

London, Printed, and Sold for *J. Morphew* near *Stationer's-Hall*. 1709.

THE PREFACE.

IT'S possible these Sheets may fall into some Hands, who in this Moderate Age, may think it too invidious a Subject to look back, and reflect, on the many Villanies, and bloody Treasons, carried on, and accomplished by the Faction in the Last Age. One year of which afforded so much Matter for our Horror and Amazement; "That a Noble Historian thinks the Memory of all its Transactions ought to be rais'd out of all Records, least by the success of it, Atheism, Infidelity, and Rebellion should be propagated in the World." The Writer therefore of this Piece thinks it necessary to declare the Reasons, which induced him to the Publication of it; least he might be thought to take delight in perpetuating Heats and Animosities, and in keeping up odious Names and Distinctions.

If the pernicious Principles of the Incendiaries of those times, had been buried with them in their Graves, or had they left the least Memorial of their Penitence behind them, then indeed Christian Charity, and Candor, would have commanded a Silence and Oblivion amongst Men: But when they shall Brave it out to their Dying Hours, and their Lives shall afterwards be deliver'd down to Posterity, as fit Examples for their Imitation and Instruction. Then whoever undertakes to lay open their Crimes, and expose their Hypocrisies, with a design to stop and prevent the ill Influence, their contagious Examples might have upon this Age too much inclined to call Evil Good, that Man transgresseth not the Bounds of Charity and

Moderation, nor offendeth against any Duties either sacred or humane.

The Writer therefore of this Pamphlet was moved with an honest Zeal and just Indignation, to find a Bold Sectarian Preacher undertake to Canonize for Saints, and Confessors, those very Men, whom the best Historians had branded with lasting marks of Infamy ;[*] and whilst their Printed Sermons still remained upon Record, as so many Monuments of their Guilt in sounding the Trumpet to War, against their Most Gracious Sovereign. Methinks it was a strange Introduction of this Age to begin it with Printed Harangues in Commemoration of those Men, whose misguided Zeal had filled the former Age with Blood and Confusion, and it was as odd a way of ushering in the Reign of our Most Glorious Queen so publickly to vindicate the Memories of those Men, who had so barbarously treated her Royal Grandfather K. Charles I. For what sincere obedience, and respect, can Her Majesty expect from those Men, who think their Names deserve to be Embalmed, who did actually represent the best of Princes, as more a Nero, than Nero himself, who pursued him with their venemous Tongues from Palace to Palace, from Camp to Camp, from Prison to Prison ; nay, at length, to the Scaffold itself ; and afterwards wrote in Defence of his Murder, calling it an Honourable Sentence, that might be justified from clear Texts of Scripture, and from the Pulpit declared his Destruction to be just and righteous ; of all which particular Accusations, some one or other of the most Dignified Saints in Calamy's Calendar were most highly guilty of.

And must not this Race of Men be for ever Factious and Seditious, if Those who rise up in their Rooms, do but imitate their Examples, and partake of the same Spirit, whereby they were acted, which is so much desired and recommended by Mr. Calamy ; Now if he would be understood only to respect the latter part of these Men's Lives, when they were silenced and ejected ; it ought likewise to be considered, that no one of these Incendiaries, howsoever guilty, did ever show the least remorse of Conscience, or Penitence, for their

---

[*] Calamy's Abridgment.

Preface. 7

former seditious Practices, but on the contrary, continued to Libel and Defame both Church and State, even after they had received extraordinary Marks of Mercy and Forgiveness; and for any one to talk of such Mens being acted with a Divine Spirit, of being guided and assisted with the Presence of God, is making very bold with that sacred tremendous Name, and is a high Profanation of Religion, and favours much of the formal Cant and Hypocrisy of the Times.

I may venture to move my Reader with Mr. Calamy to view his List of Confessors, and desire him to observe what manner of Men they were, who were the Spoils and Triumphs of Uniformity, and he will there find the very small number of Learn'd and Worthy Men, so obscured, and hid, in a Crowd of wild Enthsiuasts and ignorant Mechanicks, that he must view and review them, before he can discover them. Besides, an Impartial Observer will look back and consider, by what Methods, and by whose Patronage these Men filled the Church, and from thence be able to form a right Judgment of the Qualifications and Abilities of the Ministers, who were ejected by the Act of Uniformity. Is any thing more evident! than that Those who had the ascendency of Affairs through the whole Kingdom, made it their Business for many Years to bring an Illiterate Ministry into the Church; and that the surest way to Preferment, was, the most ready compliance to their Usurpation; now that such Tools and Little Creatures of State should become Men of such Publick Ministerial Abilities and Usefulness,* as no Age or Country have produced the like, seems a thing incredible, whether we have respect to their Educations, their Printed Discourses, or to the deplorable State of Religion, which in their Times, was nothing but Cant and Enthusiasm.

Let us take a view of the Priests and Religion of those Times from the Mouth of one of their own most noted Writers, who thus expostulates with their Reforming Parliament;† " You have done,

---

* See Hist. of England Vol. 3. p. 192.
† Preface to Edward's Gangræna.

says he, worthily against Prelates, scandalous Ministers and Ceremonies, but what have you done against other kinds of growing Evils, Heresies, Schisms, and Disorders : You have made a Reformation, but with it have we not a Deformation, and worse things come in upon us than ever we had before? You have put down the Common Prayer, and there are Many amongst us have put down the Scriptures, you have cast out Ceremonies in the Sacraments, and we have many cast out the Sacraments themselves, you have put down Saints Days, and we have Many make nothing at all of the Lord's Day ; in the Bishops Days, we had the Fourth Commandment taken away, but now we have all the Ten ; the worst of Prelates had many sound Doctrines, and had many commendable Practices, but Many Sects in our Day deny all Principles of Religion, are Enemies to all holy Duties, Order, and Learning ; in the Bishop's Days, we had many unlearned Ministers, and have we not now a Company of Jeroboam's Priests? You have destroyed Baal and his Priests, but have you been zealous against Golden Calves, and the Priests of the Lowest of the people?" This account of the Presbyterian Reformation was wrote within Four Years after the Extirpation of Episcopacy ; judge ye therefore to what an amazing height, Ignorance, Profaneness, Atheism, and Rebellion must necessarily grow in so fruitful a Soil, after many Years longer Continuance to encrease and multiply in. From hence we may learn, what various Disorders and endless Confusions we must expect, if ever the Adherers to the Puritanical Principle, of the necessity of a further Reformation in the Church, should have their Liberties to reform Religion to their Humours : Is it not highly probable, they would sit like their Westminster Assembly so long in finding out a New Religion, that at last they would leave none at all ?

But let us return to Calamy's Confessors, whom we are told were of the Lowest of the People, and like to Jeroboam's Priests ; its well, he was not of the Laudensian Faction, who gave this Character of them, for then it would have been thought horridly Censorious, and an insufferable Injury ; how often is poor Antony a Wood the

Subject of Calamy's Scorn and Reproach, because he did not think so favourably of them, as Calamy does; Mr. Wood indeed gave his Characters with great Truth and Impartiality, neither denying them their due Praises, nor industriously concealing their Faults; which is the Business of a Faithful Historian, whereas Mr. Calamy, though he gives the particular Characters of several Hundred Persons, yet throws all their Faults behind the Curtain, and wont allow of any Blemish, or Miscarriage, in any one Instance; and what makes him to be more inexcusable, is, that he only pretends to be the Abridger of Baxter's Life, who with great Freedom laid open their Faults, when he had mentioned their supposed Virtues; nay, I can instance in one memorable Name, whom Mr. B. represents as a meer State Jugler, as one who was the greatest Encourager and main Stickler in all the various Changes of the Times, and the greatest Opposer of Peace and Concord; what can be more sharp or biting, than these Reflections of Mr. Baxter's upon some of Dr. Owen's seditious Practices?* Oh! What may not Pride doe? And what Miscarriages will not false Principles and Faction hide? And taking Occasion to mention his Writings, The Doctor, says he, being neither able to repent (hitherto) or to justify himself, must be silent, or only plead the Act of Oblivion. In short, he thought the Doctor gave great Advantage to their Adversaries for Reproach, and that he occasioned a general Injury to the Nonconformists. Whereas Mr. B. faithful Abridger, is full of the Doctors Praises and Virtues, and reckons him the brightest Ornament of the Age, and one of the greatest Honours to their Cause; and then bestows some passionate Expressions on poor Antony a Wood, though he gives the Doctor a much more favourable Character than Mr. B. would allow him, the one mentioning his natural and acquired Endowments, the other having not a Word in his Favor.

There is an Instance where Mr. Calamy thought to bear hard upon Mr. Wood, but indeed betrays a strange Folly in giving so fair a

---

* See his Life Part 3. pag. 42.

Handle for an Adversary to expose him. Mr. Wood having given a particular Account of the Sermons of a Presbyterian Preacher,* he likewise tells us, that he preached the Funeral Sermon of J. Bradshaw President of the High Court of Justice, that condemned King Charles I. to Die, and that he took great Liberty in speaking much to the Honour and Praise of that Monster of Men. Now after Mr. C. has given as fulsom a Character of the Preacher, as he did of the President, he then takes Mr. Wood to Task for carping at the Preacher for this Sermon, and where is Mr. Wood's Fault? In wondring that a Preacher of the Gospel should mount the Pulpit, and there pronounce great Praises and Commendations on a Man, who durst sentence his Soveraign to Death, an Action of that barbarous amazing Nature, that the very Thoughts of it, gives a Shock to humane Nature, and put our Spirits in a Ferment; certainly the Preacher ne'er designed nor thought his Auditory could entertain an ill Opinion of Murder, Treason and Rebellion, for then they must needs have condemn'd his deceased Hero, and wonder'd at his impious Discourse.

A late Noble Historian (with all imaginable Deference be it mention'd) has not given a more notorious Instance of their Preachers perverting and wresting the Scriptures to their odious Purposes than this I am here insisting on; for Bradshaw was hired, Judas like, for Mony, was a Man of great Pride and Impudence, of a Bloody and Cruel Temper beyond all Comparison, and yet the Preacher pitched upon the following Text, as he thought most applicable to his deceased Friend, viz. The Righteous Perisheth, and no Man layeth it to Heart, and Merciful Men are taken away, none considering, that the Righteous is taken away from the Evil to come.† Now if Bradshaw was a Merciful or a Righteous Man, there never was a Cruel or Wicked Man since the Creation, and if he was not Guilty of Crimes against which Damnation it self is denounced, and Hell-fire prepared, then the most Profligate Wretch, and the most daring Sinner, that ever defied Heaven and Judgment, may hope for Mercy; and yet it

---

* Mr. Rowe.   † Isaiah 57. Ch. ver. 1.

must be owned, that had the Preacher chose only the latter Part of his Text, it might have been very fitly applied to Bradshaw's Case; for had he lived but a very few Months longer, Tyburn had been his Fate, and a Halter his deserved Punishment; so that the Preacher seem'd to have spoken prophetically, when he said, that He was taken away from the Evil to come.

We are told indeed, that Julian the Apostate and Nero, had their deserved Praises, and why might not Bradshaw have his Virtues too; It's one thing to write as an Historian, and another to speak from the Pulpit, where clapping the Title of Saint * upon a Villain and a Traytor, may very probably have a bad Influence upon the Congregation. It's very strange that Mr. Calamy can allow, that Nero had his deserved Praises, and yet wont spare one good Word in Favour of that Virtuous Prince King Charles the I. nor indeed fairly represent any one contested Action of his Life, but on the contrary, uses his utmost Art to blacken and defame his Memory, and I may safely defy him to produce any one Instance in all Mr. Baxter's voluminous Writings, where he mentions that Prince, or any of his Actions, with any tolerable respect or candor, and yet he has ventured to sanctify and defend the greatest Incendiaries, and Traytors, that any Nation was ever cursed with, and has sent them by wholesale into Heaven and everlasting Rest.

It would be endless, should I go about to enumerate all the weak and trifling Exceptions, which Mr. Calamy makes against Mr. Wood; but I can't forbear observing, how the Poor Man's Enemies are put to their Shifts and Inventions, when he is at Rest, and in his Grave, for matter, wherewith to blacken and revile him; Mr. Calamy fancies him to have been a merry boon Companion, one that was used to pass away the tedious Hours over a Glass, diverting himself and Company with wanton Tales; whereas an Oxonian Adversary, who doubtless knew him better, vents his Spleen against him after a very different manner, for he represents him to have been a melancholy monkish

---

* Calamy abridg. p. 208.

Scholar, confined to his Study, and a Stranger to Men and Conversation.*

Certainly Mr. Calamy spits his Venom against the Oxford Historiographer with a very ill Grace, when he charges him with making bitter and spiteful Reflections, which if true, only regards the Characters of a few private Persons : Whereas Mr. Calamy is very free in his Reproaches, and inveighings, against our established Laws, which the Wisdom of the Nation has provided for the Honour and Safety of our Religion, the Peace and Welfare of the Nation ; as if he had the Modesty to think that King, Lords, and Commons ought to have submitted to his Humour and Sentiments. At this Rate, the Legislative Authority may enact, what Laws they please ; but they must expect no great Regard and Reverence will be paid to them, so long as every Malapert Scribbler has the Liberty publickly to libel and censure them. "A great Man † once told the House of Commons, that it imported the very Essence of Parliaments to keep up the Honour of it's former Acts, and not to suffer them to be blasted from abroad ; believe me, says he, all the Reverence and Authority, which we expect from future times to our own Acts hereafter, depends upon our upholding the Dignity of what former Parliaments have done."

Methinks it's strange, that Calamy and those of his Denomination, can't be contented to be dispensed with for their Obedience to the Laws, but they must reproach, and libel them with a Malice always superior to their Understandings ; otherwise Mr. Calamy could never have represented Episcopal Government to have been most suitable to Ignorance, Carelessness, and Formality, ‡ nor have aspersed the Conforming Clergy, as Men, who minded Preferment more than real Religion : ‖ In short, a Pack of meer raw, unfurnish'd Novices, and yet mark the Confidence of the Man, when he says his Abridgement hath met with Acceptance amongst Men of Temper, of all Ranks and Denominations beyond his Expectation. Whereas those very Divines, §

---

* Dr. Pope in his Life of B. Ward p. 171.

† Lord Digby.   ‡ p. 48.   ‖ p. 491.   § Mr. Olliffe and Hoadly.

who have chiefly took him to Task, by refuting his Calumnies, and exposing his Malice, are Persons, who take all Opportunities to distinguish themselves for their singular Moderation to all sober Dissenters, and have jointly declared, "that they never yet knew any single Person, who did not esteem Mr. Calamy's to be an unreasonable Performance, naturally tending to revive our Differences, when the Toleration had laid this matter asleep;" and Mr. Olliffe declares, that his whole Discourse seems to him to be one continued Misrepresentation of the Terms of Conformity, by his severe and rigid Interpretations, which the Law doth not require, and when the plain Construction, and Use of Words would not only admit of, but do fairly call for another Sense without any Stretch or Force.

I cannot pass by another Instance of Calamy's great Assurance, his Prefixing the Name of a Noble Peer to his Book, which throws so much Filth and Scandal on the Royal Cause, for which the Family of that Honourable Person suffered so much, and in which they so eminently signalized themselves, and at this day so justly glory in; whereas the Dedication carries with it this impudent Supposition, that his Lordship would disown a Cause, which has given so much Honour to his Family. My Lord Clarendon has observed upon the same Occasion, That the Modesty of this Race of People is always equal to their Obedience. And that stigmatized Wretch De Foe, the Mercenary Fool and Advocate for the Party, has given us a later Instance of the Truth and Justness of our noble Authors Observation, by presuming to dedicate to her sacred Majesty his scurrilous Ribaldry, and imploring her Royal Protection to one of the most perjured and lewdest Apostates of the Age.* But when they have a publick Party Purse to maintain and support the Cause, to be sure they will never want prostitute Pens to defend it.

The Press has swarmed with scurrilous Pamphlets against the Church, and her Bishops, ever since the Reign of Queen Elizabeth, and her Historian Camden often mentions their Billingsgate

---

* Abraham Gill.

Language, being fitter for Scullions in a Kitchin, than Members of a Christian Community; and therefore must not a late Dissenting Scribler* be nearly allied to the first born of Impudence, who in the very Frontispiece of his Book avers, that the Dissenters Behaviour to the Church of England was ever most Christian; and afterwards pretends that the Rudeness at any time offered to her, proceeded from some of the vulgar People, which ought to bring no reflection on their Ministers; but Mr. Camden expressly says, that these Scriblers were of the Ministry,† and more than once complains of the strange Petulancy and sullen Haughtiness of the congregational Teachers, inspight of all the Tenderness and prudent Forbearance of the then Archbishop.

Was not the Authors of the Smectymnuan Libel of their Ministry, where they call Episcopacy an Antichristian Government, from whence Pride, Treason and Rebellion issued: Did not they revile and asperse the very pious and moderate Bishop Hall, by calling him an Arrogant, Confident, and Self-confounded Man, which as the Bishop observes, are but a handful out of a full Sack; and therefore with what Face can Mr. Palmer aver, that they never offered any Indignities to any Sober, Pious Person of the Church's Communion: But according to a new way of Writing, a Man may Libel and Defame, nay, pull down and destroy the Church and Bishops, and it must be look'd upon, as an Argument of most Christian Behavior towards them.

Mr Palmer has likewise a pretty way with him of stating the Merits of the Cause, by puting the Case of the Church upon the Level with the Dissenters, as if there ought to be the same awe and restraint upon a Man, who writes against a Pestilent Sect, or a seditious Party of Men, as when they presume to write against our established Church and Laws. I am sure, where ever they have Power, they restrain People from so much as speaking against their Church Government. They know very well, where Presbytery is so very rampant, as to

---

* Mr. Palmer. † See Vind. p. 73.

Preface.

fortunate Prince to take all occasions to aggravate every Error and Miscarriage of Government, and yet pass over in utter silence those many Gracious Acts, he so readily consented to, for the taking away all Grievances real or imaginary; Besides, the Condition of that People must be very miserable and deservedly too, that when their Properties have been invaded by their Prince, the most reasonable Securities, Concessions, and Reparations shan't be thought satisfactory, but the whole Kingdom must be set in a Flame, that their Prince may be sure to see his Error. I think we may safely conclude, that Those who argue after this manner, and justify the former Proceedings, are resolved to play the Old Game over again, whenever a fitting Opportunity serves.

The whole Prosecution of Mr. Palmer's arguing upon this Head, is one continued Series of bold Assertions; I believe he is the first Man, who called the Late Revolution* the Second Civil War, and compared the Proceedings of the Convention to the rebellious Practices of the Refuse of the Two Houses in Forty One. It's first to be observed, that if the Late Revolution was a Civil War, then King William gained his Point by Conquest, and how the Nation will receive such a Notion, may easily be guessed from the Fate of an Eminent Writer; and then most of the Proceedings of that Assembly, who took upon them the Name of the Parliament, and as such engaged War against the King, have been reversed and annulled by the whole Legislative Powers, with the highest Marks of Infamy and abhorrence; nay, both Lords and Commons since the Revolution have expressly declared their utmost dislike to the seditious Practices of those unhappy Times: And now after all this, it's very daring for any Private Person publickly to write in their Vindication, and pretend to Warrant their Proceedings upon the same Grounds, and Principles, with our Present happy Establishment; where all the Parts of our Legal Civil Power, that could then be had, joyned in the Exercise of that Provisional Power, which is necessary reserved to a

---

* P. 44.

Free People, to prevent the utter Subversion of our Constitution and the Destruction of a whole Community. But the Case of Forty One was vastly different, for then some sly and crafty Managers incensed and abused the well meaning Zealots, in order to carry on their own ambitious Designs, and at last raised their own Fortune upon the ruins of their Country, by establishing themselves in the Royal Power and Dignity, and usurping that Government into their own Hands, which by repeated Oaths they had vowed to maintain and uphold; thus we may observe, some Men who would be thought such mighty Advocates for the Revolution, become the Rankest Libellers of it.

It's likewise alleged by Mr. Palmer,* That the King was murdered, the Republick erected, and the Usurpation supported by a little Faction, and a few of Cromwell's Partizans assisted by the Army. And so, he thinks, no ways concerns the Body of Dissenters.

Mr Palmer must entertain a very weak Opinion of his Reader, when he endeavours to perswade him into a Belief, that a Small Faction, or a Few Partizans, ever did, or can destroy the Constitution of a Government, so well cemented and established as ours was, and is known to be; and then for the Army, it's strange if they did amiss, since we are assured, that they had so many pious, laborious, and worthy Divines to attend and instruct every Regiment: But it's plain, that the Frame of our old English Constitution was unhinged, the Authority and Power of the Laws defied, and trampled upon, before the Army was raised; and long before the War began, may the Parliament be said to have lost its Name, and its Nature too; for when the Iniquity of the Times are so bad, as not to permit that August Assembly to sit, speak, and vote with Honour, Freedom, and Safety, when its Debates are awed, and influenced by a Tumultuary and Menacing Rabble, when things received and settled upon solemn Debates, are resumed, altered, and determined contrary to the Law and Custom of Parliaments, then is the very Being, the vital, and essential Parts of her Constitution, sunk, and destroyed, and it's notoriously

* P. 46.

evident, that this was the true State of those Times we are speaking of; and it's a manifest Absurdity to lay these Things upon the Army, because we must suppose a thing to act, before it has a Being; and then for that unhappy part, which relates to the Person of the King, it's plain, the War only accomplished and finished his Ruin, for before that begun, a prevailing Faction in the Army had despoiled him of his Royalty, and almost reduced him to the Condition of a private Person, by robbing him of his Revenue, the Militia, and other Legal Prerogatives; and I shall show hereafter, that the barbarous Murder of that King, ought not to be laid wholly to the Charge of the Army, for they acted but one Part in that deep Villany, and so ought to bear but an equal share in the Reproach of it.

Thus have I examined, and I hope refuted too, the most material Allegations brought by Mr. Palmer in Vindication of the Dissenter's Loyalty, and most Christian Behaviour to our Church, and I shall here dismiss him with these Remarks; That he has forgot to oblige the World with his Notes on my Lord Clarendon's History, which were to give more Satisfaction than the Book it self has done: Nor must he think to come off by his mysterious way of expressing himself, That his notes should come out, when the peculiar Turn that his Lordship's Principles did oblige him to give to all the Parts in his History, were removed.* Since Mr. Palmer plainly owns, that noble History does oppose, and contradict his Assertions, nor has he paid another just Debt to Mr. Westly, who was promised some mighty Matters from Mr. Palmer's severe Studies, and which was to silence Mr. Westly from any further Demands, What have you done? But notwithstanding all these vain-glorious Boastings, the Mountain has not brought forth so much as a Mouse.

It's long ago, since it was first observed, That many had repented of Presbytery, but Presbytery never had repented of any thing; and the same Charge does at this Day stand good against them. How injurious they were to King Charles I. by casting that odious Jealousie, and groundless Aspersion on him, of his designing to reduce the whole

---

* See his Preface.

Nation to Popery, by which senseless Scandal they so much distracted the Minds of the People, and disturbed the Peace, and Settlement of the Kingdom: And when many of these Incendiaries survived the Passion and Fury of those Times, yet to the great Aggravation of their Guilt, they never repented of, or made any Reparation for their former Conduct, and not a few of them lived to see Barefaced Popery mount the Throne, and use open Violence in carrying on her Designs; and then these Men servilely courted, and thank her for the Breach of those Laws, on which our Religion and Liberties depended; and those who had been so much against Set Forms, were then content the Priests should indite for them. What they did in that Reign, says the present Bishop of Sarum, is well known, and cannot be excused.* But Calamy and Palmer, tho' they affect to quote his Lordship's Authority on many occasions, yet in this particular, they beg his Pardon, and have endeavoured to excuse, and even to justify their Addresses in that Reign. Mr. Baxter thought that some Romish Priests preached to the Independent Congregations in the Times of our Confusion, and had he not been so partial to the Presbyterians, there was the same Reasons to believe, they shelter'd and disguised themselves amongst that Sect, especially, when we are assured from good Authorities, that there was a Romish Seminary at Paris, for young Students Twice in the Week to oppose one another, one defending Presbytery, the other Independency, and one of the Learnedest of the Convent, took Notes, and judged of the Proficiency, and Genius of the Disputants, and as their Fancies lay, they were to exercise their Wits, either in Presbytery or Independency; and when they returned to England, they were taught their Lesson to say, that they were poor Christians, that formerly fled beyond Sea for their Religion sake, and were returned with glad News to enjoy their Liberty of Conscience; and we are assured,† that one Hundred of them went over in 1646. and were most of them Soldiers in the

---

* See Letter to a Dissenter, who says, that Mony was sprinkled amongst the Dissenting Ministers. P. 9.

† See Ushers Life p. 611.

SEDITIOUS PREACHERS,

UNGODLY TEACHERS.

MY Chief Design in writing this Piece being to Demonstrate, That it was seditious Puritan Preachers who stirred up the People to the Rebellion in Forty one, and were the Cause of all those Confusions in Church and State ; I think it will not be improper or foreign to my Purpose to look back and examine into the Loyalty of this Race of Men, when they first appeared in the World, whereby it will be evident, that an insolent Behaviour to Royal Authority, and an open Defiance to the Civil Magistrate were always inherent to their Principles, and that defaming of Governments with scurrilous Libels was their constant Practice, and that in despight of the Laws and the express Inhibition of the Crown, they held their Synods and their Classes, and formed their Presbyteries, and at length obliged that most Wise Princess Queen Elizabeth to punish them with Pillories and Gibbets for the Safety of her Crown and Person, and to enact Laws to suppress their outragious Insolencies, and she could never master their Confederacies and Clamours without extreme Justice ; tho' at first she hoped to quiet them by her Lenity and Forbearance, but that only served to encourage and heighten their Boldness. So that it was not any pretended Ecclesiastical Severities in King Charles I. Reign, that provoked them to rebell, and to desire the total Extirpation of Episcopacy, but a furious Zeal to have their Darling Idol Presbytery established as the Rule of Church Government and Discipline: Which they had in vain tho' often attempted in the former Reigns. And the Truth of these Assertions will most evidently appear from the Testimony of that great Statesman Sir Thomas Walsingham, who gives the following Account of the factious Zeal, which animated the Puritans of his Time.

He first acquaints us with the Queens steddy Adherence to two Maxims, the one was, not to force Consciences, the other was, not to suffer factious Practices go unpunished, because they were covered with the Pretences of Conscience; and the Queen could never be brought to deviate from these Rules, neither by the crafty Insinuations of Courtiers, nor by the bold Clamours of restless Spirits, who laboured to establish the Geneva Discipline, who as long as they only inveighed against some Abuses, it was not their Zeal, but only their Violence that was condemned, when they refused to comply with some Ceremonies, they were connived at with great Gentleness; but it was observed that they affected Popularity much, and the Methods they took to compass their Ends were judged dangerous. They set up a new Model of Church Discipline, which was like to prove no less dangerous to the Liberties of private Men, than to the Sovereign Power of the Prince; yet all this was born with as long as they proceeded with those Expressions of Duty which became Subjects. But afterwards when they resolved to carry on their Designs, without waiting for the Consent of the Magistrate, and entred into Combinations, when they begun to defame the Government with ridiculous Pasquils, and boasted of their Numbers and Strength, and in some Places brake out into Tumults; then it appeared, that it was Faction, not Zeal, that animated them, and upon that the Queen found it necessary to restrain them, yet she did it with all the Moderation, that could consist with the Peace of the Church and State.*

---

* Compare this with Palmer's Vindication, page 90. Line 9.

We find this Account recited at large in the History of the Reformation, as the most authentic Relation of the Puritans Behaviour in that Queens Reign, by which the Author seems to justify the Necessity and Expediency of the Laws, which were then made to restrain and awe the Faction ; but how that Author came to change his Mind and declaim against those Laws as severe, and a Blemish to that glorious Reign, is not so easy to be reconciled ; especially when we consider, that he had formerly complained of that Queens Successors, for not holding the Reins of Government with the like Steadiness of hand which he thinks, would have prevented the Nation (how head-strong soever) from running into those desperate Confusions, which afterwards ensued.

In this Queens Reign this dangerous Position was first broached, viz. "That if Kings and Princes refused to reform Religion, the Inferiour Magistrates or People by direction of the Ministry, might lawfully, and ought if need required, even by Force and Arms to reform it themselves." A Doctrine very repugnant to the Queens Supremacy, and tending to raise disturbances in the State, whenever their unreasonable Demands are not complied with, and it was conformable to this Traiterous Assertion, that the Assembly of Divines met at Westminster, and published their Directory in Opposition to the express Commands of their Prince.

The Judicious Mr. Hooker acquaints us, how they affirmed that their Pastors, and Elders, ought to be in the Church, whether her Majesty and the State would or not, and how they threatned, that since neither their Suits to the Parliament, nor Supplications to the Convocation prevailed, we must blame our selves, if to bring in their Discipline, some such means should hereafter be used, as shall cause our Hearts to ake ; and accordingly we find them taking Advantage of the Necessities of the Government to be the most clamorous and insulting, and when the Danger of the Crown demanded their firmest Adherence and united Strength, then a separating Spirit divided them from the Unity of their Fellow Subjects.

The Dissenters now-a-days are very fond upon all occasions to quote Father Fox the Martyrologist, and would fain have him be thought to have favoured the Puritans; but what Opinion the Good Old Man entertained of them, he freely discovered in one of his Letters, wherein he wonders what turbulent Spirit had possessed the Factious Heads of the Puritans, and complains of their Bitterness against him, for not Raving against the Church, as they did; and for his expressing himself with more Modesty and Concern for the Publick Peace, than their furious Zeal would allow of. In short, says he, they are a set of Men, who if they encrease and gather strength, I am sorry to say, what disturbances my Mind Presages, they will bring to the Nation, and how True a Prophet he has proved, let every impartial Man judge.

Upon enquiry we may find, that no Order or Quality of Men escaped their Insults, and that the Crown, the Parliament, the Bishops and the Magistrates were too often the Subject of their contumacious Impudence.

They protested to Her Majesty, that they would be no longer Subject unto the Bishops unlawful and usurped Authority, and that She maimed and deformed the Body of Christ, by maintaining the established Government and rejecting theirs.

They tell the Parliament, for their not admitting the Platform set down in their first Admonition, that it should be easier for Sodom and Gomorrha in the Day of Judgment, than for such a Court; and that if they did not abrogate the Government by Bishops, they should be in danger of the terrible Mass of God's Wrath, both in this Life and in the Life to come.

They affirm, the Queen's Council may truly be said, to delight in the Injury and violent Oppression of God's Saints and Ministers, therefore the Lord would surely visit Them with an heavy Plague.

The Council cannot possibly deal truly in matters of Justice, between Man and Man, because they bend all their Forces to bereave Jesus Christ of his Government, and at this day they have taken greater boldness, and grown more rebellious against the Lord, and his Cause, than ever they were before.

But they reserved the choicest Flowers of their Rhetorick for the Bishops, and their Government.

They openly declared, that the Laws that maintained the Bishops are no more to be accounted of, than the Laws maintaining the Stews; and then for the Bishops themselves they call them unnatural, false, and bastardy Governors of the Church, petty Antichrists, like incarnate Devils, that will lye like Dogs; and that the worst Puritan was an honester Man, than the best Lord Bishop in Christendom; and that truly great Prelate Archbishop Whitgift, a Man of great Wisdom and Moderation, who strove to bring them over to the Church with Gentleness and Forbearance, and who often interposed between them and the Gallows, Fines and Imprisonments, yet met with no suitable returns of Gratitude and Respect; and now let impartial Posterity Judge, whether he deserved this dirty Ribaldry from them.

They said, of all the Bishops that ever were in the See of Canterbury, there was never any did so much hurt to the Church of God, as he hath done, that he was more Proud and Ambitious than Woolsey, more Tyrannical than Bonner, a very Antichristian Beast, the Belzebub of Canterbury. Even Bishop Jewel that great Light and Ornament of our Church, found it necessary to vindicate himself from the spightful Calumnies, of the Puritans, by a solemn Protestation made on his Death-bed. By this we may discover the Hypocrisy of Baxter and Calamy, who in a canting Style, tells us, that had the Bishops who succeeded Jewel been like him, they had been more honoured, and that Thousands who wished for good Bishops, were on the Parliaments side. Whereas Usher, Moreton, and even good Bishop Hall were deprived, sequestred, and plundered, with the same fury and malice, as the most obnoxious Bishops were: And how can these Men say, that the Puritans hoped and Waited to see tkeir way set up, when we are assured from undeniable Authorities, and from matters of Fact, that they Resolved to carry on their designs without waiting for the consent of the Magistrate, and that they did enter into Combinations, hold their Synods, and Form their Presbyteries, which

B. and C. would blind with the Name of Secret Conferences, but this secret way of Conferencing has brought many a Man to the Gallows, and within the Compass of the Law. If I should rake together all the Rebellious Principles, Seditious Practices, and Billingsgate Language of the Puritans in Q. Elizabeth's Reign, it were enough to fill many Volumes; whoever consults Whitgift and Bancroft's Writings, with Cambden's History, will wonder at the Superior Confidence of those Men, who now-a-days can publickly avow, that the Puritans always carried themselves with that Patience, Modesty, and Submission as became Christians, with the most exact Loyalty, and no manner of Opposition.

When King James I. removed from Scotland, to take Possession of the Imperial Crown of England, the Satisfaction he might reasonably entertain of enjoying greater Honours, Power, and Authority, cou'd not be more agreeable to his Mind, than his happy Deliverance from the insupportable Tyranny of the Scottish Presbytery, and from the Subjection to the ill manners, and insolent Practices of their Preachers, whose furious Heat had drawn Tears from him in his tender Years, and thought it their Honour to be always contending with him, whom no Deserts could oblige, no Oaths or Promises bind, and that which so much heighten'd their Boldness, was their resolute Adherence to this safe Rule, That the King, nor his Council had any Authority to judge of Treasons deliver'd in the Pulpit, but their Assemblies ought to take Cognizance thereof; and so whenever any of them was cited before the Council, the rest made it a common Cause, and complained that a wrong was done to the Kingdom of Christ, and would refuse to censure them, nay so much as to remove a Preacher to another Congregation, that the King might not hear himself rail'd at to his Face, or possibly some dire Woe denounced against him. To give a remarkable Instance.

When the King found the Death of his Mother was intended, he gave Orders to the Ministers to remember her in their publick Prayers, which they refused to do, tho' the Prayer was most Christian, and Lawful, and at the Request of their Sovereign, and on behalf of their Sovereign, and on behalf of his Royal Mother. The King had appointed the Bishop of St. Andrews to pray before him upon that melancholy Occasion, the Ministers hearing of it, stirred up a young Man, not entred into the Function, to take the Pulpit, and exclude the Bishop, which the King finding at his Coming, call'd to him from his Seat, and told him, that Place was appointed for another; however, if he would remember his Mother in his Prayers, he might stay and proceed, which he refusing to do, the Guards pulled him down, whereupon he burst forth into bitter Expressions against the King, and then denounced a Judgment against the Inhabitants of Edinburgh.

Another Preacher, in his Pulpit, denounced the Curse against the King, that befel Jeroboam; that he should dye childless, and be the last of his Race. Upon which he was brought before the Council, where he confessed the Words, and proudly maintain'd them.

One of them, in his Pulpit, had called our Renowned Queen Elizabeth an Atheist, and a Woman of no Religion; upon the Complaint of the English Ambassador, he was cited before the Council, whereupon the Commissioners of the Church appeared in his Behalf, and declared, That if the Preacher should submit his Doctrine to the Tryal of the Council, then the Liberties of the Church, and the spiritual Government of the House of God would be quite subverted, and when some few diswaded them from his seditious Course, the greater Number cried out, It was the Cause of God, whereunto it concerned them to stand at all Hazards, and accordingly, the several Presbyteries subscribed a Form for the greater Confirmation of their Doings, and recommended the Cause in hand to God in their publick Prayers, and used their best Credit with their Flocks, for the Maintenance thereof. My Historian observes, that they would yield more to the Desires of the meanest People, than to the most reasonable Propositions of their King. Nay, so much were these Godly Ministers troubled with the Spirit of Opposition, That when the

King appointed a Thanksgiving, they would proclaim a Fast, and observe it too.

Now I will give my Reader an Instance or Two, how much these Ministers countenanced and incited the People to Rebellion, and were the only Trumpets to War. The King being surprized by some Lords, and closely confined, the Ministers were so far transported with Joy upon the King's Restraint, that they could not contain themselves within any Bounds, but went up the Streets of Edinburgh, after the manner of a Popish Procession, singing the 124 Psalm; and at their next General Assembly they ratifyed and approved of the King's Imprisonment, which was afterwards adjudged Treason by the three Estates of the Realm; at last the King found means to escape out of their Hands, but they would not allow him to be long at Ease, for the Ministers encouraged the People from their Pulpits to joyn with Bothwell, who was gathering Forces to invade the King, nor did their Folly and Madness stay there, but they gave those very Monies to the levying of Soldiers for Bothwell's Rebellion, which they had collected in their Churches for the Supply and Relief of the Protestants at Geneva then under great Troubles and Distresses.

These Proceedings of the Ministers obliged the King to offer certain Articles for their Subscriptions, *viz.* that all Preachers should yield Obedience; that they should not publickly revile his Majesty; that they should not draw the People from their due obedience to the King; that they should not alledge the Inspiration of the holy Spirit, when they should be accused of their seditious Sermons and Discourses; and yet the King could not obtain any Subscriptions from their Hands to these Points, which tended so much to secure the Honour of our holy Religion, the Welfare of the King, and the happy Settlement of the Kingdom.

I think it needless to insist upon the strict Correspondence, and the sweet Harmony, between the English and Scotch Disciplinarians, and how they afforded mutual Assistance, Refuge and Protection to each other, when ever they fled from the Hands of Justice, because our

Histories are so full and clear to those Matters; and besides I hasten to bring my Discourse nearer to my intended Design. No wonder, when King James came to England, that the Episcopal Clergy so readily obtained his Favour and Protection; here he found a learned moderate, and truly religious Ministry, there he had left a violent and factious one, who employed all their Study and Care, how they should best seduce and pervert the People from their Allegiance to him. And he very well knew, that the English Disciplinarians had often pressed their People with the Example of Scotland, and endeavoured to inveigle them into a good Opinion of their Proceedings and Platform, and had certainly brought the Nation into as great Confusions as ever Scotland was cursed with, had a Prince of tender Years wore the Diadem, or an easy Princes swayed the Scepter, but Queen Elizabeth's watchful Eye and strict Hand observed and broke all their Measures, and quashed all their Violence without any Noise or Tumult.

The King conceived that some of the Scottish Ministers might be moved by force of reason to quit their Opinions, and give Place to Truth, sent for several of them to Court to hear our Learned Bishops preach, where it grieved them to the Heart, says Spotsworth, to hear the Pope and Presbytery so often equalled in their Opposition to Sovereign Princes, The King endeavoured to gain these Men by easie and Gentle Methods, sometimes appointing publick, and often condescending to private Conferences with them, but it must be acknowledged an Error in his Government, that he loosen'd the Reins, which Queen Elizabeth had kept strict upon their Necks; for she was taught by Experience, that the Power of good Laws, and a steddy Administration of them, was the only effectual way to reclaim their turbulent Spirits; we dont find King James made any Examples of his Justice by some necessary Executions, as the Queen did, and yet the Dissenters in our days ungratefully reproach him, as laying the Foundation of all the Miseries they have since endured: but I believe, that if he had pelted them with sharper Weapons than Apothegms, he had subdued those unruly Tempters, which were at last so headstrong, as to overthrow both Church and State.

We are sensible enough of their Endeavours to blacken the Memory of that Prince, and why they wont look back and insist upon the Proceedings of Queen Elizabeth's Reign towards them, for then People would be rightly informed and understand, that both King James, King Charles and Archbishop Laud used less severe means, and exercised fewer Acts of Power against them, than that the Queen had done before them, and so the implacable Hatred and the odious Reflections they are continually throwing upon those great Men, would be more obvious and exposed than they desire.

And those who are conversant in the History of those times must be sensible of the very great Disadvantages which Archbishop Laud in particular laboured under to recover the Honour and Purity of the Church, to restore it's former Orders, which had been so long neglected under the Jurisdiction of Abbot, who had been promoted to the See of Canterbury at the earnest Importunity of a Scotch Favourite; and that Archbishop was as Ignorant of the true Constitution of the Church of England, of the State and Qualifications of the Clergy as his Scotch Patron; to Abbots holding the See of Canterbury so many years, the Church in some Measure owed it's Downfal; for it was he who filled it with so many Judas's, who betrayed it into the Hands of her Enemies, who persecuted those Hands which ordained them; these were the Episcopal Men, whom Mr. Baxter and others have so often upbraided us with, who composed the Assembly at Westminster, and were accounted the Honour of the Parliaments Cause, but indeed the Disgrace and Reproach of their Mother Church, whom they had undutifully forsook in her greatest Extremity, and whose treacherous Apostacy made her the easier Prey to her more open Enemies.

We are told by the Noble Historian, that if Bishop Andrews or Overal had filled the See in Abbots room, they had quickly extinguished all that Fire in England, which had been kindled at Geneva, and that Infection would easily have been kept out, which could not afterwards be so easily expelled ; whereas Abbot made his House a Sanctuary to the most eminent of the factious Party, and licensed their most pernicious Books, and how much Envy, Malice, and ill Will must it needs bring to his Successor, when he laboured to retrieve the Antient Discipline of the Church, and to rescue her out of the Hands of weak and more false Men ; and it was the hard Fortune of that truly great and learned Prelate Archbishop Laud to succeed so unskilful a Pilot, who had run the Church upon Rocks and Shoals, and left her exposed open and defenceless to the Darts of her Enemies, and when he thought to bring her back into Haven, and to rescue her from his Predecessors Errors and Mistakes, to call them no worse, he soon found Peoples Tempers violent and impetuous, and their Insolence by former Indulgence, unbridled ; insomuch that the most necessary Reproofs and Censures were thought insupportable Injuries, and his honest Zeal in maintaining the Church, her Liturgy, Rites and Ceremonies in Decent Order and Oeconomy, was adjudged by a deluded Age a Design to introduce Popery, though his Learned Writings against the Jesuit ought to have set him beyond the least Suspicion. But his Enemies did not really think him a Friend to Rome, but an Enemy to Geneva, for the same day they adjudged him to dye, they voted out our Liturgy to make room for the Geneva Discipline.

It was King Charles the I. steddy Adherence to Episcopacy, and not giving way to their earnest Importunities for the abolishing of it, that was the Principal Cause of the great Rebellion against him, the first Tumults that were stirred up against him, proceeded from a religious Account, the Scotch raised Forces, provided Arms, and entred into solemn Leagues, and Bishop or no Bishop was the greatest Part of the Controversy ; for we must understand, that the King had set his heart upon a Uniformity of Worship thro' the whole Kingdom of Britain, and therefore had ordered a Lyturgy conformable to the English one for the Kingdom of Scotland, where King James his Father had got Episcopacy established by the Parliament, and the Assembly at Perth has made seueral other advances towards an Uniformity with England, and there seemed only to want the Liturgy to compleat the Union ; but what Reception it met with, what Tumults they raised to oppose it, I suppose, few Men are ignorant of, nor of the more outragious Behaviour of their Kirk, which obliged the king to dissolve them, however they continued to sit, and declared Episcopacy unlawful, cited their Bishops before them, and pretended Authority to Unbishop them. They likewise voted down the Book of Canons and the Articles of Perth, tho at that time established Laws of their Kingdom, and which had been ratifyed by a former general Assembly, they denied the King his Negative Vote, or Power to meddle with Ecclesiastical Affairs, alledging, that the King took upon him that Spiritual Power, which properly belonged to Christ as only King and head of the Church, the Ministry and Execution whereof was only given to such as bear the Ecclesiastical Government of the same. Now when we consider the Constitution of their General Assemblies, we shall equally admire at the Folly and Iniquity of this Doctrin. There were about 260 Commissioners, and from every Presbytery 3 or 4 Assessors, and from some Places 24 Lay Elders to one Priest, all which Lay Elders have as great Power in Matters of Doctrin and Discipline as the Priests themselves to judge and pass definitive Sentences ; and the present Bishop of Sarum assures us, That some of their Commissioners could neither write nor read, and yet they were to judge of Heresy, and condemn Arminius his Tenets.

However the Scotch Nation enter'd into Solemn Leagues and Covenants to justify and defend the Proceedings of this Motly Assembly, who threatned their Opposers with Excommunication, nay with Damnation it self, and to give it the greater Authority, Cant an eminent Presbyterian Preacher, assures the People in a Sermon preached at Glasgow, that he was sent to them with a Commission from Christ to bid them Subscribe the Covenant, which was Christs Contract, and the Bishop of Sarum informs us, that the Ministers inflamed the Nation into a War against their King by their Fasts and Prayers, and their odd Application of the Scriptures.

Now its Foreign to my present Design to show by what dishonourable Management a Treacherous Peace was clapt up, insomuch that all Men who had contributed to it, were ashamed of it, and its enough to say that this Peace laid the Foundation of all our future Miseries, all things being left with Circumstances very disgraceful to the King to be settled by a Parliament, which was to be called in a short time to meet at Westminster.

The prevailing Party in the House of Commons soon discovered a great Disaffection to Episcopacy and the Church, partly in compliance to the Scots, who quickly desired the House there might be an Uniformity of Religion between the Two Nations, for which Advice they had the Thanks of the House, and to this end they received and justified a Petition, from the Refuse of the People, that Episcopacy might be abolished Root and Branch, and resolved upon the Question, that the Judicial Power of Bishops in the House of Peers ought to be taken away, and accordingly ordered a Bill for that Purpose. They troubled and punished those Divines, who had been most Zealous for Conformity, and chose out Men of known and avow'd disaffection to the Established Church to Preach before them.

By what I have already said, I easily conjecture that my Reader will be before-hand with me in supposing that the Dissenters and Puritan Conformist would not loose this hopeful opportunity, to set up their darling Idol and pull down the Church, and by what vile contrivances, and base methods, they did actually gain their Ends, shall be my next business to show.

It has been already remark'd, that it was the Refuse of the People, who Petitioned for the abolishing Episcopacy Root and Branch ; but the Heads, Hearts, and Hands of their Clergy were the main Springs, which moved and set it on Foot, and indeed the Petition medled with very abstruse Points in Divinity, too sublime for Mechanick Heads; not a Patent or Monopoly granted, nor the Price of any Commodity raised, but these Men made Bishops the Cause.

"A Late Noble Historian informs us at large of their great disingenuity in procuring these Petitions, the Course was, first to prepare a Petition very modest and dutiful, for the Form; and for the Matter not very unreasonable; and then to communicate it at some Publick Meeting, where care was taken it should be received with Approbation: The Subscription of very few Hands filled the Paper itself, where the Petition was written; and therefore many more Sheets were annexed, for the reception of the Number, which gave all the Credit, and procured all the Countenance to the Undertaking; when a multitude of Hands was procured, the Petition itself was cut off; a new one framed, suitable to the Design in hand, and annexed to the long List of Names, which were subscribed to the former: By this means, many Men found their Hands subscribed to Petitions, of which, they before had never heard of; as several Ministers whose Hands were to the Petition and Declaration of the London Ministers before-mentioned have Professed to many Persons; That they never saw that Petition before it was presented to the House, but had signed another, the Substance of which was, not to be compelled to take the Oath enjoyned by the new Canons; and when they found instead of that, their Names set to a desire of an Alteration in the Government of the Church, they with much trouble went to Mr. Marshall, with whom they had intrusted the Petition and their Hands; who gave them no other Answer, but that it was thought proper by those who understood Busines better than they, That the latter Petition should rather be preferred than the former; and when he found, they intended by some publick Act to vindicate themselves from that Calumny; such Persons, upon whom they had their greatest dependence, were engaged, by threats and promises to prevail with them, to sit still, and to pass by that indirect Proceeding."

And Bishop Hall had an eye to this base Practice, when he tells the Parliament, if that Underhand way of procured Subscriptions could have reason to hope for favour in their Eyes? But alas, they so far prostituted the Honour of their House to these Wretches, that when they Petitioned against Bishops Votes, they ordered their Speaker to give them the Thanks of their House; and the Royal Martyr complains that at last they commanded and over-awed the very Parliament; for they usually came down in a most tumultuous manner, that their confluence and clamour might prevail. "It cannot be remembered without horror, that this strange Wild-fire amongst the People was not so much, or so furiously, kindled by the Breath of the Parliament as of their Clergy, who both administered Fuel, and blowed the Coals in the Houses too; These Men having crept into, and at last driven out all Learned and Orthodox Men from the Pulpits, had from the beginning of this Parliament, under the Notion of Reformation, infus'd seditious Inclinations into the Hearts of Men against the Government of the Church, with many libellous Invectives against the State too, and as freely inveighed against the Person of the King, as they had against the worst Malignant, profanely, and blasphemously applying whatsoever had been spoken, and declared, by God himself, or the Prophets against the most wicked and impious King, to incense and stir up the People against their most Gracious Sovereign."

Thus they had recourse to their old way of libelling and reviling, casting odious aspersions upon the Bishops, as void of Truth as of good manners, by taxing them with favouring Papists and Popish Doctrines, whereas those Prelates who felt the severest Marks of their Rage and Malice, had spent their Time, their Strength, and their Studies, in Preaching and Writing against Popery, and would have Sacrificed all the Remains of their old Blood for the Maintenance of the Protestant Religion.

Then they insinuated, that the Bishops designed to introduce Innovations into the Church, when those things the Prelates then attempted to settle for the keeping up Decency and Order in the Church, have been since thought necessary, and are now quietly established into Custom, which shows how ill designing Men and Leaders of Factions can improve things and affright People with Shadows.

But above all they taught weak People, that the Prelates countenanced and avowed Arminius's Points, and discouraged the Preaching up the Doctrines of Predestination, of Free Grace, Election for Faith foreseen, and such like mysterious Theological Tenets, above the Thoughts and Conceptions of the most learned Part of Mankind; and it was strange, it should be made a matter of complaint to the Parliament, that the Clergy were faint-hearted, and fearful of Preaching their Congregations into Despair, by continually buzzing into their Ears, that God from all Eternity had reprobated and decreed them to Damnation, these things gave occasion to our famed Hudibras to Sing,

> That hard Words, Jealousies and Fears,
> Set Folks together by the Ears.

We cannot suppose the Bench of Bishops, which then abounded with so many learned and able Pens, were so far wanting to their own Innocence, as not to vindicate themselves from these senseless and false Calumnies, No! We find the very pious Bishop Hall attempting to put a stop to the Inundation of base and scurrilous Libels, and in an humble Remonstrance to the Parliament, he intreats them to check the daring and misgrounded Insolence of the Libellers, and complains that the Press had of late forgot to speak any Language, other than libellous; and therefore begs them to consider, what a shameful injustice it was in those bold Slanderers to cast upon the zealously religious Prelates, famous for their Works against Rome in foreign Parts, the Guilt of that, which they have so meritoriously and so convincingly opposed; and then in a Treatise at large, he asserted the Divine Right of Episcopacy, and offered his Reputation to Shame, and his Life to Justice, if any Man living could shew any one Lay Presbyter, that ever was in the Christian World, till Farell and Viret first created him, which was 1500 Years after the first Propagation of the Christian Religion.

One would have thought, that the superiour Worth, Learning, and Moderation of this aged Bishop would have Protected him from all rude Assaults, especially from those who would be thought Ministers of Christ, and Preachers of the Gospel; but no sooner had this great Prelate presented his humble Remonstrance to the Parliament, but Five of their new fangled Divines attack him under the Name of

Smectymnuus in such a scurrilous manner : That as Cambden observed of the old Puritans, the Authors seemed rather Scullions out of the Kitchin, than followers of Piety.

They could find no better Name for his Learned Arguments, than calling them a heap of confident and groundless Assertions ; they tell him, he sinned deeply against the Rules of Honesty, which in plainer, but as true English, was calling him Rogue and Rascal. They likewise tell him, he acted with a Face of confident Boldness, and not only forgot himself, but God also, and that he uttered Words bordering upon Blasphemy. But let us have done with this sort of Language, fit only to drop from their Pens, whose Ink was as bitter as Gall, and venemous as Poison. I shall only observe, that these Smectymnuuan Zealots at that time overcome with the Tyranny of an ignorant Zeal ; lived to see the Nation deliver'd from the Confusions they had brought upon it, and then they desired to be thought Men of the greatest Temper and Moderation, and not they, but some few Sectarian Divines from New England were the only Incendiaries; but for them weak Lambs, they were always for moderate Episcopacy, and good Bishops : However, the Wisdom of the Nation thought it necessary at the Restoration of the Church and State, to lay some Restraints upon their Libellous Tongues, to secure their Establishment and Perpetuity, and had they not cause enough to fence against future Crimes ?

It may not be amiss to examine the particular Characters, that Calamy gives to some of these Smectymnuan Zealots, by which it will appear, that he only considered how to draw the Character of an humble good Christian in general, and then clapt the Name of one of his Confessors to it, without any Regard to the paaticular Actions, Temper, or Writings of the Man : Thus Doctor Spurstow (whom he takes care to let you know, was one of the Authors of Smectymnuus) is distinguish'd by him for his meek, humble, and peaceable Disposition ; now is not this very absurd ? First to own him to be an Author of a most seditious and scandalous Libel, and then call him a very humbly and peaceable Man. My Lord Clarendon gives us a singular Instance of this Mans great Meekness and Humility, when he very fiercely told the King to his Face, That he would be damn'd, unless he consented to the utter abolishing of Episcopacy, and behaved himself with that Rudeness, as if he meant to be no longer subject to a King, no more than to a Bishop; and our noble Author adds, that he lived after the Return of King Charles II. and according to the Modesty of that Race of People, came to kiss his Majesty's Hand, and continued the same Zeal in all seditious Attempts.

The next Character is that of Old Calamy, who tho' he was in his Judgment for the Presbyterian Discipline, yet he was of known Moderation towards those of other Sentiments, and that he was very Active to an Accommodation, and was one of those, who met in the Jerusalem Chamber with several Bishops, in which Meeting, by mutual Concessions, things were brought into a very hopeful Posture. Now he owns him to have been one of the Authors of the above-mentioned Libel, which certainly contradicts his pretended peaceable and accommodating Temper, for that Book was wrote on purpose to subvert the established Church, and as they themselves have boasted gave the first deadly Blow; not to insist on the vile and unchristian Treatment, which the truly moderate Bishop Hall met with from their Hands, and then if we may give Credit to old Calamy's own Testimony, we have it from his own Mouth, that he was the chief Instrument in framing and encouraging the Root and Branch Petition, for he boasts that it was formed in his House before the Beginning of the long Parliament. Now mark the Villany and Hypocrisy of this Man, he meets the Bishops in the Jerusalem Chamber, in order to accommodate Matters, and pretends to them to be of an healing Temper; when at the same time, he had a Petition in his Pocket to desire the Parliament totally to abolish the established Government of the Church, which was delivered, and had their wished for Success. With the same Air of Truth we are told, that this Man kept his Temper and Moderation after his Ejectment, whereas he was the very first Man, who committed any open Violation to the Act of Uniformity, and suffered for it accordingly.

Thus from these Two contradictory and absurd Characters, we may make a Judgment of the Rest, and know how to credit little Calamy's Relations both of Men and Things.

It was the Votes and Resolutions of the House of Commons, which animated the seditious Party, and added Life and Vigour to their outragious Insolencies; for at the Beginning of the Parliament, the Puritan Faction published a Sham Order in the Name of the House of Commons assembled in Parliament, to stir up and invite Active Men to accuse Ministers, which Order (tho disclaimed within the Walls of the House, yet they had not Virtue enough to countermand it, nor to enquire into the Publishers of it,) occasioned many Petitions against the Clergy; for if any Knave or Fool bore any ill Will to his Minister, or did not care to pay his Tyth, he presently got Two or Three base Mechanicks to sign a Petition, which constantly run in the Name of the whole Parish, tho Three Parts in Four had never seen it, but disowned it under their Hands, then it was no hard matter to procure false Witnesses; for said they, the Parliament put no man to his Oath, nor give any Costs or Damages upon Default of Proof; and so many a Clergyman, after a chargeable and vexatious Attendance, and sometimes Imprisonment, has been dismissed from their Committees, without so much as reproving the false Witness, or censuring the malicious Accuser.

And it often happened, that a Minister was called upon to answer for some Doctrinal Points he had preached perhaps Twenty Years before, as many were for saying, That Baptism washeth away Original Sin, and one was for saying, That the Blessed Virgin was the Mother of God; then must he give a Fee to a common Lawyer to plead for him at the Bar of the House, and prove the Soundness of his Doctrine.

A Complaint was made to the House, that Doctor Couzens endeavored to seduce a young Student to embrace Popery, and that his Friends were obliged to remove him from the College to prevent it; whereas the Doctor made it appear by several Members of their own House, that he being Vicechancellor of Cambridge, upon Examination,

F

found the Party Mr. Nichols guilty of holding Popish Tenets, whereupon he made him publickly recant his Popery, and then expelled him the University.

In some Cases they betrayed their great Malice, and notorious Ignorance, Doctor Stern was charged with Blasphemy, for only writing round the Bason for gathering Alms, Honour God with thy Substance.

Indeed, Mr. White the Chairman of the Committee published a List of scandalous and malignant Priests, which he called his first Century, being the Names of one hundred Divines sequestred for scandalous Enormities; and the Enemies of our Church at this day reproach us with this black List, and appeal to it to justify the Parliaments Proceedings, to throw all possible Scandal on the Clergy of that time; but whoever slightly looks over that List, will soon discover great Malice and Disingenuity in the Publisher, for of the Hundred Instances he produces, Malignancy against the Parliament, or a Neglect of some of their Orders is an objected Crime against more than Fourscore of them, and yet the only Design of the Publisher was, (as appears by his Preface,) to represent the Body of the Clergy as Men of vitious Lives and scandalous Conversations, and that the Prelates who ordained them into the Ministry were justly deprived, and their Government in the Church with great Reason abolished. But in Truth, Confotmity to the Church, and Loyalty to the King, made these Ministers so obnoxious to their Faction, who had waged War against the King, and appointed Monthly Fasts to be observed for the Success of their Arms, and it's a main Article against many in this List, that they did not religiously observe these Fasts in their Churches; and then they requir'd them to take the Covenant to capacitate them to hold their Livings, where they swear with all Sincerity, Reality, and Constancy, to defend and preserve the King's Majesties Person; now to keep this Oath, and yet to fast and pray for the Success of those Men, who were then firing in the Face of the King, was such a Contradiction, as the evading Pens of a Baxter or Calamy can't reconcile: These were those Blessed times, when swearing was a Sin, but forswearing a Duty; for when Mr. White required Dr. Featly to take the Covenant, he refused, and alledged that it was contrary to his Oath of Allegiance to his Sovereign, and contrary to his Oath of Canonical Obedience to his Bishop; whereupon White told him, he must suffer and be turned out, to which the good Man replied, "Nec mihi ignominiosum est pati, quod pasus est Christus, nec tibi gloriosum est facere, quod fecit Judas." And its no Wonder, that White dyed distracted in the midst of his Rage against the Church, crying out, how many Clergymen, their Wives and Children he had ruined.

Reader, think it not strange, that I undertake to demonstrate from this truly scandalous List, that the Clergy of this time was generally Men of Vertue and unexceptionable Lives and Conversations; Mr. W. in his Preface tells his Reader, he should have an Essay of the Gall and Wormwood of the Episcopal Government taken out of London the Metropolis, and by that he should see, what Vermin crawled upon and devoured the principal and vital Parts.

Now there are 123 Parishes within the Bills of Mortality, and yet we find but 7 Names recorded in this formidable List, who belonged to those Parishes, and of that very small number, some were not taxed with the least Immorality; one was for only writing a Book, to prove it Sacrilege to take away the Lands of Deans and Chapters, and that the Parliament perverted the Will of the Dead that gave them. Others was, for expressing great Malignancy against the Parliament, which indeed was the Burthen of the Song through the whole List. Now if the London Clergy, who were immediately under the watchful Eye of the Parliament, had so trifling a Number liable to their severest Scrutiny; I think we may safely conclude, that the Prelates of that time had taken great Care to fill the Churches of London with Men of great Piety and unexceptionable Lives. Besides Bishop Juxon and his immediate Predecessor Laud were acknowleg'd by their greatest Enemies to have been Men of Eminent Piety and strict Manners, who sure would never have suffered a debauched and careless Clergy to have disgraced their Diocese.

I shall farther observe, that there was 115 Ministers sequestred and turned out of the 123 Parishes above mentioned, which shews how little regard ought to be had to what Baxter, or his Abridger, relate for certain Truths, for they both averr, that those who were sequestred were proved insufficient and scandalous; and that those who were cast out for the War alone, as for Opinion sake, were comparatively few.

But it may be objected in Answer to this, that Mr. Baxter has elsewhere affirmed the contrary, and at a time too when he may be reasonably supposed to have spoken his Thoughts more freely; for he tells us in his holy Common-wealth, that the Parliament displaced many in the Universities upon the Account of Religion, and that they cast out abundance of Ministers upon the same Account. Whoever is the least conversant in Mr Baxter's Life and Conversation, knows that Richard and Baxter were continually mortifying one another. However the Slips of a Treacherous Memory are far more excusable, than the bold Assertions of notorious Falsities, for Mr Baxter more than once affirms that White published two Centuries of scandalous Ministers, which is a Falsity as black and malicious as the Assertions and Scandals he intended thereby to throw upon the Church and her Ministers.

A noted Author, who lived and wrote in the Heat of the Rebellion, mentions Whites first Century, but avows, that to his Knowledge there never came forth a Second, and that when some solicited his Majesty for Leave to set forth a Book of the vicious Lives of some Parliament Ministers, his Majesty blasted the Design, least the Common Enemy the Papist might take the Advantage of it. And I never could find upon the strictest Enquiry, that any one ever saw this second Century. But Mr. Calamy tho' an Abridger, is yet more particular in this matter than Mr. Baxter, no doubt it was to show his Readiness to publish any Slanders that might blacken the Episcopal Clergy; for he tells the World, that White, or the Chairman of the Committee was the Publisher of a Century of scandalous Ministers, which was afterwards followed with a second Century, both filled

Sedition against his own Person and the Peace of the Kingdom, that he was many times amazed to consider by what Eyes those things were seen, and by what Ears they were heard.

The Dissenters now-a-days would have us believe, that the War begun upon a Civil Account, but sure those that lived in that time knew best upon what Grounds they took up Arms, and incited others to do the like, and that it was for the Cause of Religion, and Reformation, will most evidently appear from the following Considerations.

When the Parliament was to borrow Mony of the City to carry on the War, they employed the Ministers to Harangue the Citizens assembled at Guild-hall, with the seasonableness and necessity of their being liberal in their Contributions, in order to preserve their Religion then in imminent danger. It was upon one of these Grand Solemnities, "that old Calumy a loud Trumpeter to War, gave his Mighty and Omnipotent Arguments to perswade them to a Liberal Contribution, but at the same time raised this very Pertinent Objection, Why should the Ministers engage themselves so much in this Business? Why, says he, to procure a Religious Peace, that may continue the Gospel amongst us, and bring a Reformation, such as all the Godly in the Kingdom desired; he tells them they might easily have a French Peace, that would bring a Massacre with it; (which was a bold Intimation that the King designed it) and then goes on to justify his own conduct, by informing them, that the Priests in the Old Testament sounded the Silver Trumpets to War; and if this was the way of God, certainly much more in such a Cause as this, where Religion is so intwined, and indeed so interlaced, that Religion and This Cause like Hippocrates his Twins, they must live and dye together. And Gentlemen, says he, if Religion were not concern'd in this Cause, and Mightily concerned to, and if Religion did not live and dye with it, We had not appeared this day; and then least they should be faint-hearted, and pretend they were exhausted with their continual Demands, our Divine tells them, that Jesus Christ emptied himself of his Divinity to make us rich, and shed his Blood for them; you have not yet made your selves so Poor as

Jesus Christ was, that had no House to lodge in, and he did all this for your sakes; you have not yet shed your Blood for the Cause of Christ: We read that Moses was willing to be blotted out of the Book of Life for the Cause of God, and will you not venture your earthly Provisions for so Good a Cause as this. Religion hath produced all your Wealth you have, all your Wealth is but the Child of Religion, (tho' it was ten to one but many of his Auditors got their Wealth by Sequestring, and Oppressing, the Kings most faithful Subjects) and then I hope your Riches will preserve Religion; and let me assure you on the Word of a Minister, the contributing to this Cause for God's sake; for the Glory of God, and for the Peace of the Gospel, will be a means to make you the sooner ascend up Jacob's Ladder, not for the giving the Mony, but for the Evidence of your Faith, through the Merits of the Lord Jesus Christ, by your giving of the Mony; happy Mony, that will purchase the Gospel, Religion, and Reformation to our Posterity, and I count it the greatest Opportunity, that ever God did offer to the godly of this Kingdom, to give them some Money to lend to this Cause, the Lord give you Hearts to believe this (and we find great was their Faith, for the City at that time contributed a very large Summ to carry on the War) and here is an Extraordinary Appearance of so many Ministers to encourage in this Cause, that you may see how real the godly Ministry in England is unto this Cause, and I speak in the Name of these Reverend Ministers, that we will not only speak to perswade you to contribute, but every one of us have already lent and will lend to our utmost Power."

"Inter Folia Fructus."

The Massacres

OF

SAINT BARTHOLOMEW.

"History is but the Unrolled Scroll of Prophecy."
—James A. Garfield.

PRIVATELY PRINTED
FOR THE CLARENDON HISTORICAL SOCIETY.

1888.

This edition is limited to 120 *large paper and* 400 *small paper copies, for Subscribers only.*

The Massacres

OF

SAINT BARTHOLOMEW.

24TH AUGUST—5TH SSPTEMBER, 1572.

AT this time, when people who ought to know better, are endeavoring to obscure the terrible truth of this unequalled religious crime, perpetrated by the Papalists upon the Protestants of France, it is well for the descendants of those who suffered, many in our midst, to recall its unsurpassable horrors. It was not done in a hurry or in a corner, and a medal lies by the writer's side, brought out from Rome by a distinguished Italian patriot, which was prepared by the order of Gregory XIII. to commemorate this "Slaughter of the Huguenots." It is not an original, because such were impossible to obtain while the Papal government held Rome, but it was struck from the original die, ordered by Pope Gregory XIII., whose effigy is on the obverse, with his name, titles, &c.

The reverse shows an angel (*sic*) with a sword in his right hand, elevating the cross with his left, while before him and at his feet lie the murdered French Huguenots or Protestants. This reverse bears the legend, "*Ugonottorum Strages*, 1572." There are other facsimiles in this city and they are now to be found dispersed abroad, although, until recently, buried and unattainable.

What was perpretrated in Paris alone, can be found in so many works, there is no need to repeat the horrible story of the thousand upon thousand of murders which commenced on the 24th of August, 1572, and continued to strike down the best of Frenchmen through so many bloody days and weeks. What occurred in the provinces is not so well known.

Let us examine these!

If the decree of the secret council for the extermination of the Protestants encountered no obstacle in the capital—Paris—such was not the fact, in some cases, in the provinces. Several cities escaped the common disaster through the courage and wisdom of their magistracies and military authorities. Others (this includes the great majority) were given up to pillage and to devastation, and the spectacle of the massacre of their best citizens.

MEAUX, 25 MILES E. N. E. OF PARIS.

The Queen Mother (Catharine) was Countess of Meaux and had therein numerous and devoted partisans. This city had been the cradle of Protestantism. We are translating, as a rule from a French work known as "The Dictionary of Conversation," published in Paris, in 1833, and the author of the article under consideration is Dufey (de l'Yonne). This writer is one of the voluminous contributors. The Bishop of Meaux, Briconnet, at first adopted and publicly professed the reformed (Protestant or Huguenot) doctrines, and gathered around him a number of distinguished theologians who shared his views. Among these were Jacques Lefevre and William Farel, subsequently distinguished as Protestant divines.

Briconnet, however, was less of a zealous propagandist than an ambitious courtier. Accordingly, by an astounding change of front, he deserted his party, and, to win his pardon from the court for what he styled his errors, he became the most pitiless persecutor of the religion for which he had previously shown the most lively devotion.

His abandonment of his friends was the cause and prelude of bloody collisions. As soon as the plan of extermination had been definitely resolved upon by the secret council, and the hour of execution determined, a messenger was despatched to Meaux. He was accompanied by Lefroid, a ferocious member of the Romanist league, and was accredited to Louis Cosset, the Royal Procurator, or attorney. This Bosset at once assembled all the robbers and murderers who had rendered themselves conspicuous by their fanaticism and their ferocity since the commencement of the French civil wars. He fixed a place for their assembling the very same day, at 7 P.M. All were to be armed and ready to fall upon the Protestants. At the same hour the gates of the city were shut. Cosset chose for associates to engineer the execution, Denis Roland, an usher or tipstaff, "a man worthy of a thousand gallows for his robberies and his exactions;" Pigeon, a bargeman; and some priests. They divided their followers into bands, who commenced by seizing and imprisoning the Protestants and then pillaging their dwellings. The massacres did not occur until the morrow, but continued for three days. The women and girls were violated and then murdered. The Protestants who were in the country about, and those who sought a refuge there, escaped neither pillage nor death.

***

Troyes, capital of Champagne, 90 miles E. S. E. of Paris.

The news of the massacres in the royal city arrived in Troyes on the 26th of August. The Romanists at once fell upon the Protestants and the pillaging, the murders, continued for nine days (4th September.) The victims who sought asylums in the houses were followed thither without pity, tracked like wild beasts and massacred.

ORLEANS, 58 MILES S. S. W. OF PARIS.

The announcement of the murderous decree reached this city on the 26th of August and at once the imprisonments and the robberies began. The number of Protestants murdered is set down at 1,200. This does not comprise fifty women and many little children. The massacres and the havoc lasted three days. Some Protestants escaped from the city. Certain of the magistrates, accomplices of the assassins and robbers, devised an expedient, which, in a measure, enticed the fugitives back into Orleans. They caused an amnesty, entire and without restriction, to be made public, in favor of all those who would return to the (Roman) church. Some unfortunates, in the hope of saving their lives and their properties, resolved to abjure their faith to a Cordelier (Fransciscan friar) designated by the proclamations to receive them. These unhappy men were none the less robbed and murdered. "These '*Little Massacres*,'" says a contemporary historian, "lasted fifteen days."

BOURGES, 123 MILES S. OF PARIS.

In this city, as in almost every locality where the Leaguers were masters, massacres were executed with the same circumstances; closure of the gates of the city; imprisonment of the Protestants; pillage of their property. The blood continued to flow for many days. The band of assassins were led by Boirat, captain of the Burgher militia, his brother, an Echevin (somewhat like an assistant alderman), a member of the municipal government and other fanatics belonging to the same family: Montjan—sword cutler, Ambroise—shoemaker, Yves Camaille—butcher. All the Protestants imprisoned in the course of the 26th and 27th of August were pitilessly massacred.

LA CHARITE, N. E. OF BOURGES ON THE LOIRE.

The company of the Duke of Nevers, composed of Italians, marched into this city the very day of Saint Bartholomew, 24th of August, and halted there under pretext of being reviewed. The officers had received secret orders from the Duke of Nevers. Soon afterwards these foreign soldiers united with the Leaguers, attacked and pillaged the houses of the Protestants. The rich of this party were subjected to heavy ransom. On the 3d of September massacres began and continued for many days.

SANCERRE, N. E. OF BOURGES, IN THE DIRECTION OF LA CHARITE.

The Protestants who had escaped from the massacre in Orleans, in Bourges, and in La Charite— a sad misnomer for a place destitute of brotherly love—took refuge at Sancerre, whose population was almost entirely Protestant, and combined with them for their common defense. Their calm and determined attitude surprised and frightened the Romanists, so that the latter did not dare to attack them. The Protestants, although most numerous, did not take advantage of their superiority. They would not permit any reprisals, thus to deprive their persecutors of every pretext for summoning to their assistance the troops of the Duke de la Chatres, who had received orders to repair to Sancerre. They always showed themselves in public in large numbers and perfectly organized, but without ostensible weapons ; so as not to violate the last Royal edict, which prohibited carrying arms ; which edict was intended to deprive the Protestants of the means of defending themselves. Almost all the towns of Brittany, west-north-west province of France ; of Anjou, capital Angers, to the south-east of this ; and of Saintonge, more southerly again, were theatres of the most frightful disasters.

LYONS, the second city of France, was, after Paris, the most unfortunate of municipalities. Mandelot, the governor, who was a partisan of the Guises, had orders to accomplish the extermination of all the Protestants, without distinction of age or sex. At first he hesitated to execute this infernal order with all its intended rigor.

He confined himself to ordering the gates of the city to be closed, and imprisoning the Protestants under pretext, thus, of placing them under the protection of the magistrates and of the public force (police) and thereby saving them from the popular fury. This, however, amounted to nothing, since he charged the Burgher militia with the arrest of the intended victims. This citizen organisation summoned to its aid all the Romanist Leaguers of the country, and these escorts, assigned under the pretence of safeguards, led their prisoners into bystreets, murdered them there and then cast their corpses into the Rhone. The bands of cut-throats were under the direction of one Boidon, an assassin and robber by profession—a wretch who subsequently terminated his horrible career on the scaffold, at Clermont, in Auvergne. These pillages and massacres had already lasted three days, when, on the 29th of September, arrived from Paris de Perat, decorated with the Royal Order of Saint Michael and bearer of letters from Queen Catherine. With him was associated one de Rubis, and several Echevins (assistant aldermen?) of Lyon, who had been sojourning some time in Paris, attending to the interests of the Lyonese merchants. The letters confided to de Perat announced in effect, that the King desired that Lyon should imitate the capital; that all the Protestants should be exterminated. The governor, Mandelot, alleged that he was every hour expecting direct orders from the king. At the same time, however, he published a notice that all those who professed the Reformed religion must repair without delay to the government hall. These unhappy people thereupon hastened to place themselves under the safeguard of the military authority. La Pierre d' Auxerre, Advocate Royal, declared that the King and the Queen Mother ordered the extermination of all the Protestants, not only those already in Prison, but all those who could be arrested. For this he produced no written authority. Nevertheless Mandelot yielded to his arguments and soon after Bordon, Mornieu and Le Clou, companions in the debaucheries, and comrades in the crimes of La Pierre, proposed to the public executioner to associate himself in their enterprise. This grim functionary, however, had more humanity than his superiors. He boldly told them "that he performed his functions simply in executing the sentences of the magistrates and that he would not sully his office by the massacre of innocent people." The soldiers in the citadel made a like reply to a similar proposition from La Pierre and his fellow-villains : "What you demand is against honor. We are not assassins. What evil have these unfortunates done, that you wish us to slaughter them?" The murderers were thus compelled to purchase the services of some bandits and the Guards of the City Hall (composed of 800 Burgher militia). These they divided into bands and by them, all the Protestants, confined in the convents of the Franciscan and Celestine monks, were murdered.

The principal merchants who professed the Reformed religion, had been shut up in the palace of the Archbishop. The Leaguers first imposed heavy ransoms on them, and, notwithstanding, killed them afterwards. Mandelot and Saluces hurried to the palace of the Archbishop to stop the slaughter, but they were too late. Mandelot, in order to evade the terrible responsibility of this massacre, hastened to prepare an accusation setting forth the facts, directed against the actual authors of this crime. He promised a hundred crowns of gold to whoever would produce proofs of their guilt. This ostentatious demonstration of indictment and of reward made no impression on the criminals. They were sure of impunity. Their fury redoubled, and on the evening of the very same day that these official documents appeared, they repaired to the prison of Roanne, crowded with Protestants, fastened cords to the necks of these, dragged them to the Rhone and threw them into the river. The courts of the archepiscopal palace were filled with corpses. Mandelot had them conveyed to the opposite side of the river, in order that they might be interred in the Cemetery of the Abbey d'Aulnay, but the monks set their faces against it, under the pretext that these heretics were unworthy of burial. Then the members of the League, at a concerted signal, themselves removed the heaps of dead and cast them into the Rhone. "The bodies of the fattest were given over to the apothecaries." The number of victims exceeded 800. The lives of two ministers and some Protestant laymen were saved by Saluces, commandant of the citadel.

The Rhone cast ashore the corpses thrown into it. These encumbered the environs of Tournon, Valence, Bourg, Vienne, Le Pont de St. Esprit, Avignon, Arles, &c., towns along its course to the sea. The authorities were obliged to compel the boatmen with their boat-hooks to shove back the dead bodies into the Rhone, and for a long time the riparian populations would neither eat of the fish of the river, nor make any use of its waters.

VALENCE, on the left bank of the Rhone, and ROMANS, 10 miles to the north-east, on the right bank of the Isere. In both these towns some Protestants were murdered; but their fellow-worshippers were saved by the courageous firmness of Simiane de Cordes.

Claude of Savoy, of Tende, who commanded in DAUPHINY, refused to execute the orders of the Secret Council which were brought to him by Boniface de la Motte. To this court emissary, he made this noble reply: "It is impossible that such orders could have originated with his Majesty. They must have been conceived by enemies to the throne and public tranquility; by people who prostitute the name of the King in order to gratify their passions." This generous refusal cost him his life. He died of poison administered to him at Avignon, a city belonging to the Pope.

BAYONNE, EXTREME S. W. OF FRANCE.

The Viscount d'Orte, governor of this city, took the wisest and most energetic measures to restrain the Romanist Leaguers. No

Protestant was attacked. To the orders of the King he likewise made a memorable answer: "Sire, I have communicated the commands of your Majesty to your faithful citizens and men-at-arms constituting the garrison. Among them I have found none others but good citizens and brave soldiers, and not a single executioner. For this reason both they and myself very humbly supplicate your Majesty to be pleased to employ our arms and our lives in things which are possible, however dangerous they may be. For such we place ourselves at your disposal, even to the last drop of our blood." This refusal to obey unjust and sanguinary orders likewise cost his life to this brave citizen. He died poisoned a short time afterwards; and the government of Bayonne was given to the Count de Retz, a creature of the Secret Council.

AUVERGNE.

The Protestants of this province escaped extermination solely through the devotion of Saint-Heran, its governor, who had the courage to imitate the generous refusals which the Count of Tende and the Viscount d'Orte opposed to the royal command.

DIJON had only reason to deplore a single victim, Clermont de Traves, brother-in-law of the Count of Grammont. Advantage was taken of the absence of Charny, who commanded in this city, to kill this Protestant gentleman.

MACON.—The Protestants were almost all put in prison. The governor, Philibert de la Guiche, adopted this measure to save them and it was successful. The prison served as a veritable and secure refuge for the unfortunates destined to the knife; and this brave governor was able to make their enemies respect his determination.

NISMES, in Languedoc, afterwards, in 1815, like Avignon and other towns in the south of France, the scene of bloodthirsty bigotry, won, on the other hand, in 1572, an honorable record. Its Romanist inhabitants did not share the atrocious frenzy of the Leaguers, and themselves rallied to the defence of the Protestants. They united with the latter for the common maintenance of order in the city, and, therein, the orders of the Secret Council were not executed.

ROUEN, NORMANDY, 68 MILES N. W. OF PARIS, ON THE SEINE.

Tannequi-le-Veneur, the governor of this city, at first resisted, not only the instigations, but the menaces of the Leaguers. Very soon, however, his authority ceased to be recognized. The numerous Protestants who inhabited this vast and populous city were shut up in prisons on the 17th of September, 1572. The cut-throats assembled in arms before the prison, forced their victims to come forth, one after another, and murdered them. The number of victims ranged between 800 and 900. All their houses were pillaged. As for the corpses, they were first stripped of their clothing; this, by an affectation of piety, was bestowed upon the poor. Then the bodies were thrown into large holes dug for the purpose, outside the gate de Caux. The provincial parliament promulgated a sentence against the robbers and assassins. But this decree was nothing but a cruel and scandalous piece of deceit. These murders of the Protestants at Rouen in 1572, were a perfect type of the massacres of Paris by the Jacobins in 1791. In both cases the victims belonged to the best classes of society and the cut-throats to the worst.

TOULOUSE, Languedoc.—Infamous in 1762 for the judicial murder, of the Protestant Calas, which roused the indignation of Europe, this city was the stage of the last act of the long tragedy of desolation and of crime. The massacre of the Protestants of this city closed her lists of the crimes of Saint Bartholowew. Duranti, Advocate General, was accused of having given a frightful signal for the murder of his fellow-citizens. He was afterwards promoted to be First President of the same provincial parliament to which he had been attorney-general. Subsequently, when desirous of opposing new aggressions of the very Leaguers of whom he had been the accomplice, he perished, together with Dassis, his brother-in-law, assassinated by them in 1589. His corpse was wraped up in the canvas of a grand picture representing Henry III., who hnd incurred the hatred of members of the League in consequence of his alliance with the Protestant Henry of Navarre, afterwards Henry IV.

Michelet mentions selling the bodies of fat Protestants to apothecaries.

History has consecrated the names of the magistrates, of the governors, of the military commanders, of the citizens, who glorified themselves by their heroic resistance to the orders of the Secret Council—good men, who here and there in different cities and some in the provinces, saved a portion of the population, their innocent fellow-citizens, so unjustly proscribed.

Truth and justice requires the mention of the following noble men, in addition to those already cited as exceptions to the general list of ferocious instruments of royal and priestly infamy : M. M. Sonagues at Dieppe (North); the Count of Garces in Provence (S. E.); the First President of the Parliament of Grenoble (E.) ; President Jeannin, at Dijon ; Villars, at Nismes ; the Marshal de Matignon, at Alençon; de Rieux, at Narbonne ; Curzas, at Angers ; Bouillé, in Brittany ; Henuyer, Bishop of Lisieux; all the Montmorencies throughout their vast dominions, and in the towns and cities wherever they held commands.

Salignac-Fenelon, then French Ambassador at London, received orders to justify these massacres to Queen Elizabeth. His bold and honorable answer to his king, Charles IX., came near costing him dear. He was threatened with a severe punishment for making it. "Sire," were his words, "I should render myself an accomplice of this terrible deed, if I attempted to excuse it. Your Majesty must address yourself to those who counseled the execution."

Even the massacre of St. Bartholomew has found apologists; moreover, refutations have not been wanting. Such discussions or excuses simply imply a total ignorance of the epoch. Opinion is now definitely fixed in regard to this capital crime, its origin, instigators, motives, method and iniquity.

A French officer justly characterized it as worse than a crime. It was a blunder; followed up by worse blunders, if less meanly sanguinary crimes. The Revocation of the Edict of Nantes and its consequences completed the list. These deviltries of bigotry continued for over 200 years and were most disastrous to France. In driving out the Huguenots, they drove out industry, economy, knowledge, honesty and thought—the origin and stimulant of progress. The revulsion of the Revolution was the necessary consequence of the centuries of such crimes. The rulers set the example and demoralized the people. In like manner the utter depravity of the imperial rule of Louis Napoleon generated the excesses of the Commune. The pendulum never ceases to vibrate, nor the application of the law of compensation, even in this world. The cruelty towards the Huguenots and their expulsion was the source of the calamities of France in 1870.

The Huguenots furnished nerve and brain to Prussia.. Frederick the Great was their pupil in all that made him truly glorious. When Prussia succumbed in 1806, it was Huguenot blood which mitigated the fall. The first Prussian general who fell on French soil in 1870, bore a Huguenot name. It is claimed that when the victorious Germans rode into Paris in 1871, eighty descendants of Huguenots rode in the staff of the triumphant Emperor who had so much to avenge and avenged it. The same race inspirited the United States of Holland; gave sap to the early manhood of this city; helped William the Third to the crown of Great Britain and performed leader's and yeoman's work in his military successes. What is more, the greatest French admiral who ever shed glory on the Bourbon

"Inter Folia Fructus."

AN ORDINANCE

Appointing

COMMISSIONERS

For Approbation of

Publique Preachers.

Printed by William du Gard and Henry Hills, printers to His Highness the Lord Protector.
1653.

"History is but the Unrolled Scroll of Prophecy."
—James A. Garfield.

PRIVATELY PRINTED
FOR THE CLARENDON HISTORICAL SOCIETY.

1889.

An Ordinance Appointing Commissioners for Approbation of Publique Preachers.

Whereas for some time past hitherto there hath not been any certain course established for the supplying vacant places with able and fit persons to preach the Gospel, by reason whereof not one of the Rights and Titles of Patrons are prejudiced, but many weak, scandalous, popish, and illaffected persons have intruded themselves, or been brought in, to the great grief and trouble of the good people of this Nation ; For remedy and prevention whereof, Be it ordained by his Highness the Lord Protector, by and with the consent of his Council, that every person, who shall from and after the five and twentieth day of March instant be presented, nominated, chosen, or appointed to any Benefice (formerly called Benefice with Care of Souls) or to preach any public settled Lecture in England or Wales, shall, before he be admitted into any such Benefice, or Lecture, be judged and approved, by the persons hereafter named, to be a person for the Grace of God in him, his holy and unblamable Conversation, as also for his knowledge and utterance, able and fit to preach the Gospel ; And that after the said five and twentieth day of March, no person, but such as shall upon such approbation be admitted by the said persons, shall take any publique Lecture, having a constant stipend legally annexed and belonging thereunto, or take or receive any such Benefice as aforesaid, or the profits thereof ; And be it further ordained, That Francis Rous, Esq.; Dr. Thomas Goodwin, Dr. John Owen,

Mr. Thankful Owen, Dr. Arrowsmith, Dr. Tuckney, Dr. Horton, Mr. Joseph Caryl, Mr. Philip Ny, Mr. William Carter, Mr. Sidrach Simpson, Mr. William Greenhill, Mr. William Strong, Mr. Thomas Manton, Mr. Samual Slater, Mr. William Cooper, Mr. Stephen Marshal, Mr. John Tombes, Mr. Walter Cradock, Mr. Samuel Faircloth, Mr. Hugh Peters, Mr. Peter Sterry, Mr. Samuel Bamford, Mr. Thomas Valentine of Chaford, Mr. Henry Jeffee, Mr. Obadiah Sedgewick, Mr. Nicholas Lockier, Mr. Daniel Dyke, Mr James Russel, Mr Nathanael Campfield, Robert Tichborn Alderman of London, Mark Hildesly, Thomas Wood, John Saddler, William Goff, Thomas St. Nicholas, William Packer, and Edward Creffet, Esquires, shall be, and are hereby nominated, constituted and appointed Commissioners for such approbation and admission as is abovesaid, and upon death or removal of any of them, others shall from time to time be nominated in their places by the Lord Protector and his Successors, by advice of his Council, in the Interval of Parliaments, and sitting the Parliament, by the Protector and Parliament; And the said Commissioners, or any five or more of them, met together in some certain place in the City of London or Westminster, as his Highness shall appoint, are hereby authorized to judge and take knowledge of the ability and fitness of any person so Presented, nominated, chosen or appointed according to the qualification abovementioned, and upon their approbation of such his ability and fitness, to grant unto such person admission to such Benefice or Lecture by an Instrument in Writing under a Common Seal to be appointed by his Highness, and under the hand of the Register or Registers for the time being to be also nominated by the Lord Protector and his Successors, which Instrument the said Register or Registers shall cause to be entered in a Book for that purpose, and kept upon Record.

And it is hereby declared, That the said person so admitted into any such Benefice, shall be Possessors and Incumbent of the same, and intituled thereby to the Profits, Perquisits, and all Rights and Dues incident and belonging thereunto, as fully and effectually as if he had been instituted and inducted according to the Laws of this Realm; as also the person that shall be so admitted to any Lecture as aforesaid, shall be thereby enabled, according to the establishment and constitution of such Lecture, to preach therein, and to have and receive the Stipend or Profits to such Lecture belonging.

Provided alwaies, That no person who shall tender himself, or be tendered, for approbation as aforesaid, shall be concluded by any vote of the said Commissioners which shall pass in the Negative as to his approbation, unless nine or more of the said Commissioners be present at such Vote.

And it is further Ordained, That all Patrons of any Benefices that are now void, shall within six Moneths next after the five and twentieth of this instant March, and of any Benefice that shall hereafter be void within six Months next after the avoidance of the same, Present unto the said Commissioners, or any five of them, some fit person to be admitted, and for default of such Presentation within that time, the Presentation for that turn shall devolve by lapse unto the Lord Protector and his Successors.

Provided alwaies, That in case the Patron be disturbed to Present unto such Benefice, and thereupon within six moneths after the avoidance of such Benefice a Suite be commmenced for the Recovery of such Presentation, and notice thereof in writing left with the said Commissioners, or any five of them, or the Register, that then such notice shall be as effectual to prevent the lapse, as where the sute was heretofore commenced against the Bishop or Ordinary.

And it is further Ordained, That during the vacancy of such place by reason of such State, the said Commissioners, or any five or more of them, have hereby authority to sequester the fruits and profits thereof for supplying of the place with an able Preacher, by the said Commissioners, or any five or more of them, to be nominated and approved of as aforesaid.

And forasmuch as many persons since the first day of April last past have been placed in such Benefices, and publique Lectures, It is hereby Ordained, That in case such person shall not before the four and twentieth day of June next, obtain approbation and admittance in the manner before exprest, Then such person or persons as have right thereunto shall or may Present or nominate some other fit and able person to such place.

And in defalt of such Presentation within two Moneths after the said four and twentieth day of June, or within six Moneths after the place became void, the Presentation for that turn shall likewise devolve by lapse unto the Lord Protector and his Successors.

And for the better satisfaction of the said Commissioners touching the godly and unblameable conversation of such persons as are to bee admitted in any place as aforesaid, It is further Declared and Ordained, that before any admittance of any person as aforesaid, there shall bee brought to the said Commissioners, or any five of them, a Testimonial or Certificate in writing, subscribed with the hands of three persons of known godliness and integritie, whereof one at least to bee a preacher of the Gospel in some constant settled place; Testifying upon their personal knowledge the holy and good conversation of the person so to bee admitted : which said Certificate shall bee dulie Registered and filed. And it is also declared, that all penaltie for or in respect of the not subscribing or reading the Articles mentioned in the Act of the 13th yeer of Queen Elisabeth, Intituled, Reformation of Disorders in the Ministers of the Church: or for not producing such Testimonial as in the said Act is required, shall from henceforth cease and be void.

And whereas for the better maintenance of preaching Ministers, several Augmentations by Authoritie of Parliament have been heretofore granted, Bee it further Ordained, that all person or persons, who claim or shall hereafter claim the benefit of such Augmentation, shall before hee or they receive the same, obtain the approbation of the said Commissioners or five of them, as a person qualified as is before mentioned. And in case of approbation, such approbation shall be entred by the Register, who under his hand shall also signifie the same to such person or persons as are or shall be authorized to pay such Augmentation, Who are hereby required and authorized from time to time to pay the person or persons so approved, such Augmentation as hath been or shall bee granted unto him or the place where hee preacheth, taking his or their Aquittances for the same. Provided, and it is hereby Declared, that this Ordinance or any thing therein conteined, shall not bee construed to extend unto, or to revive any dignities, offices or benefices Ecclesiastical, suppressed by Authoritie of Parliament. Nor of any benefices Ecclesiastical that were not presentative before the Ordinance for suppression of Bishops : Nor to any Lectures preached or read in any of the Universities.

And it is hereby lastly Declared and Ordained, That the Approbation or admittance aforesaid, in such manner as is before prescribed, is not intended nor shall bee construed to bee any Solemn or Sacred setting apart of a person to any particular office in the Ministrie : But onely by such trial and approbation to take care that places destitute may be supplied, with able and faithful Preachers throughout this Nation. And that such fit and approved persons faithfully labouring in the work of the Gospel, may bee in a capacitie to receive such public stipend and maintenance, as is or shall bee allotted to such places.

HEN. SCOBEL,, Clerk
of the Council.

20. *March*, 1653.

ORdered by His Highness the Lord PROTECTOR and His Council, That this Ordinance bee forthwith Printed and Published.

HEN. SCOBEL, Clerk
of the Council.

www.ingramcontent.com/pod-product-compliance
Lightning Source LLC
Chambersburg PA
CBHW020237090426
42735CB00010B/1732